Dear Parent:

Congratulations! Your child is taking the first steps on an exciting journey. The destination? Independent reading!

STEP INTO READING® will help your child get there. The program offers five steps to reading success. Each step includes fun stories and colorful art. There are also Step into Reading Sticker Books, Step into Reading Math Readers, Step into Reading Write-In Readers, Step into Reading Phonics Readers, and Step into Reading Phonics First Steps! Boxed Sets—a complete literacy program with something for every child.

Learning to Read, Step by Step!

Ready to Read Preschool–Kindergarten
• big type and easy words • rhyme and rhythm • picture clues
For children who know the alphabet and are eager to begin reading.

Reading with Help Preschool–Grade 1
• basic vocabulary • short sentences • simple stories
For children who recognize familiar words and sound out new words with help.

Reading on Your Own Grades 1–3
• engaging characters • easy-to-follow plots • popular topics
For children who are ready to read on their own.

Reading Paragraphs Grades 2–3
• challenging vocabulary • short paragraphs • exciting stories
For newly independent readers who read simple sentences with confidence.

Ready for Chapters Grades 2–4
• chapters • longer paragraphs • full-color art
For children who want to take the plunge into chapter books but still like colorful pictures.

STEP INTO READING® is designed to give every child a successful reading experience. The grade levels are only guides. Children can progress through the steps at their own speed, developing confidence in their reading, no matter what their grade.

Remember, a lifetime love of reading starts with a single step!

For Nancy, whose enthusiasm is magic
—M.K.

With grateful acknowledgment to Sid Radner, honorary curator,
and Matt Carpenter, curator of collections,
of the Houdini Historical Center, Appleton, Wisconsin,
for their time and expertise in reviewing this manuscript.

Photo credits:
Photographs courtesy of the LIBRARY OF CONGRESS Prints and Photographs Division.
Page 36, reproduction number LC-USZ62-11234DLC,
page 47, reproduced from the Collections of the LIBRARY OF CONGRESS,
page 48, reproduction number LC-USZ62-112431DLC.

www.stepintoreading.com

Educators and librarians, for a variety of teaching tools, visit us at
www.randomhouse.com/teachers

Library of Congress Cataloging-in-Publication Data
Kulling, Monica.
The great Houdini / by Monica Kulling ; illustrated by Anne Reas.
    p.   cm. — (Step into reading. A step 4 book)
SUMMARY: An introduction to the life of Harry Houdini, one of the most famous magicians
of all time.
ISBN 0-679-88573-0 (trade) — ISBN 0-679-98573-5 (lib. bdg.)
1. Houdini, Harry, 1874–1926—Juvenile literature.
2. Magicians—United States—Biography—Juvenile literature.
3. Escape artists—United States—Biography—Juvenile literature.
[1. Houdini, Harry, 1874–1926. 2. Magicians.]
I. Reas, Anne, ill. II. Title. III. Series: Step into reading. Step 4 book.
GV1545.H8   K85   2003   793.8'092—dc21   2002015695

Printed in the United States of America   13 12

THE GREAT HOUDINI

by Monica Kulling

illustrated by Anne Reas

Random House 🏠 New York

Chapter One

Every summer, the circus came to Appleton, Wisconsin. Nine-year-old Ehrich Weiss loved the acrobats and the magicians. He wanted to be a performer.

"I will call myself 'The Prince of the Air,'" he told his brother Theo.

Ehrich made a trapeze out of a broomstick and two ropes. His mother sewed him a costume. He looked like a real acrobat. Soon he was ready for his first performance!

The neighborhood kids gathered to see the show. Ehrich and Theo had made a stage. An old sheet was used as a curtain. Ehrich ran out from behind the curtain. He grabbed the trapeze and began to swing back and forth. He stood on his hands. He hung by his knees.

Then it was time for his best trick. Theo stuck needles in the ground. Ehrich swung over the needles. He picked up every single one—with his eyelids!

Ehrich Weiss was born in Budapest, Hungary, in 1874. Soon after, the whole family moved to America. His father was a rabbi. He didn't make enough money to feed his large family.

Ehrich and his brothers did odd jobs to earn money. Ehrich ran errands, sold newspapers, and shined shoes.

He decided to quit grade school. In those days, there were no laws to make children stay in school. Ehrich needed to help his family. He got a job in a locksmith's shop.

Ehrich learned to take locks apart and put them back together. He also learned to open locks by using a pick made of wire. Soon he could open *any* lock in the shop—without a key!

Chapter Two

Ehrich was fascinated with magic. He read every book on magic he could find. He learned coin and card tricks. He even learned how to escape after being tied up with rope.

One of Ehrich's favorite books was about the French magician Jean Eugène Robert-Houdin. Ehrich was thinking of him when he made up his stage name. He added an "i" to "Houdin." Then he changed his nickname, "Ehrie," into "Harry." And so "Harry Houdini" was born.

While still in their teens, Harry and Theo put together a magic show. They called themselves "The Brothers Houdini." They pulled coins and cards out of thin air. They turned a candle flame into a handkerchief.

Harry practiced his hand movements for hours on end. "Quicker than the eye can see," he told Theo.

The Brothers Houdini always saved the best trick for last. It was called Metamorphosis, which means "change." Harry would change into Theo.

Harry tied Theo in a sack. Then he locked him in a trunk. He placed a curtain in front of the trunk. Harry went behind the curtain. At the count of three, the audience saw *Theo* move the curtain—and *Harry* jump out of the trunk!

The trick was so quick, people could not guess how they did it.

They took their act on the road
and ended up in New York City. Harry
and Theo got a job performing at an
amusement fair on Coney Island. Here,
Harry met Bess Rahner. She was
performing in a song and dance act
with her sister.

Harry and Bess fell in love. They were
married in 1894. Bess took Theo's place in
the act. It was the end of the Brothers
Houdini.

Theo went on performing as a solo
magician. He called himself "Hardeen." But
he never became as famous as his brother.

Chapter Three

Harry and Bess struggled for years to find work. Finally, the Welsh Brothers Circus in Pennsylvania gave them a six-month contract.

The Houdinis put together some new tricks. They added touches to their famous Metamorphosis illusion. Harry entered the trunk handcuffed. Bess emerged from the trunk wearing Harry's coat.

Harry's ability to pick locks came in handy for handcuff escapes. He also knew that some cuffs opened when they were hit on a hard surface. He tied a piece of metal to his knees, hidden under his pants. When he smacked the cuffs against the metal, the cuffs "magically" snapped open.

Soon handcuff tricks were a regular part of Houdini's act. He always escaped easily. But the audience never seemed amazed.

"I don't get it," said Harry to Bess one day. "I'm locked up tighter than Fort Knox. And I bust out in seconds! I make it look easy."

"Maybe it looks *too* easy," replied Bess.

From then on, Houdini did the handcuff escapes inside a cabinet with only his head showing. He took his time.

He groaned and sweated and strained.
Then he burst out waving the cuffs.

The audience went wild! Now they
loved seeing Houdini break free.

Houdini added a straitjacket escape to his act. A straitjacket has very long sleeves. It is put on backward. The arms are crossed in front and tied behind. A belt is buckled around the waist.

The escape was hard work. Houdini had to undo the buckle from inside. He had to get the sleeves over his head. For almost anyone else, it would have been impossible. But not for the Great Houdini!

Once, the straitjacket escape took
Houdini over an hour! He rolled all over
the floor.

He jerked and wrestled with the jacket.

When he was finally free, Houdini's
body was bruised and sore.

"The pain and agony of that struggle
will live forever in my mind," he said later.

Houdini spent up to eight hours a day working on new escapes. But no matter how hard he worked, Houdini was not yet a star. And that's what he wanted most of all.

In 1900, Houdini bought two steamship
tickets. He and Bess were bound for
England. They hoped this move would
bring the stardom Houdini was seeking.

Chapter Four

Houdini and Bess didn't know anyone in London. They had no bookings. They had only enough money to last them one week!

Houdini went to every theater looking for work. Finally, C. Dundas Slater, the manager of London's best music hall, booked the Houdinis for a week. But soon they were out of work again. There were too many handcuff-escape artists in England.

"Now, if you could break out of cuffs from Scotland Yard," Slater told Houdini, "I could give you steady work!"

Houdini never let a challenge go by. He was ready and willing to try.

Scotland Yard was the headquarters of the London police. Criminals knew that it was impossible to break out of a jail cell in Scotland Yard—or to crack the cuffs that were used. But Houdini knew that two keys could open most British cuffs. And he owned both of them!

Houdini was handcuffed to a stone pillar inside a cell. He was checked for hidden keys. But the police could not find any. Houdini had hidden the key where no one would think to look. He'd swallowed it and was holding it in his throat!

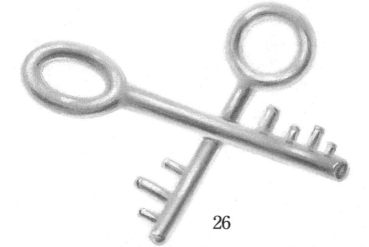

"You won't be going anywhere, I'm sure," said Superintendent Melville as he closed the door with a smile.

But Melville was wrong. In seconds, the handcuffs clattered to the floor. Houdini was free! It was unbelievable!

The Houdinis got a six-month booking. The show sold out every night. The Houdinis became the talk of London.

When the six months were up,
Houdini got work in Paris, France.
He came up with a dangerous stunt to
get people's attention. He would jump
into the river Seine—handcuffed!

A large crowd gathered. Handcuffs were locked on Houdini. His wrists were chained. Two men helped him climb a ladder to the highest pillar on the bridge.

Houdini balanced on top of the pillar. Suddenly he threw himself into the muddy river. The waters closed over him.

Seconds went by. The crowd held its breath. Then Houdini popped up, waving the cuffs. He had done the impossible once again!

Houdini and Bess toured Europe for five years. Their shows became more and more popular. When he came back to America, Houdini was world-famous!

Chapter Five

Houdini bought a huge house in New York City. It had two rooms just for his library. He had over 5,000 books on magic!

Houdini was a big star now. He took his show across the country. He toured from Boston to New Orleans to San Francisco.

In those days, there was no television. Today, when a magician such as David Copperfield goes on TV, he becomes famous overnight. It took Houdini years and years of traveling and performing all over the world to become famous.

Houdini was not the only escape artist touring the country. He needed to keep his show exciting. He wasn't going to be second to anyone!

Houdini came up with a new underwater stunt. He called it the Water Torture Cell.

A glass cabinet full of water stood on the stage. It looked like a phone booth. Houdini's ankles were locked into a wooden brace. He was then lowered into the water—upside down!

The cabinet was locked with a steel lid. A curtain was pulled in front.

Three minutes later, Houdini was free. But the cabinet was still locked! How did he do it?

The Water Torture Cell escape was Houdini's most famous stunt. He never told anyone how he did it. He liked to keep his secrets to himself.

Chapter Six

Houdini had always kept himself in great physical shape. But now he was over forty years old. The escapes were getting harder to do. He began to put magic tricks back into his act.

But these illusions were bigger than the ones he used to do. Houdini's "biggest" magic trick of the time was the Vanishing Elephant trick. He performed it for the first time in 1918 in New York City.

"Ladies and gentlemen!" Houdini shouted. "Please welcome Jenny!"

Jenny the 10,000-pound elephant tromped into the ring. She wore a wristwatch on her left hind leg.

Fifteen men wheeled out an eight-foot-square cabinet. It was big enough to hold an elephant!

Jenny was led into the cabinet. Houdini pointed at the watch on her back leg.

"Jenny keeps good time," he told the audience. "She will vanish in two seconds."

The doors were closed. Houdini counted to two. He opened the doors. *Presto!* The cabinet was empty. Jenny had vanished into thin air!

The audience loved this wonderful trick. It became one of Houdini's most famous illusions.

Houdini still performed a few of his old escapes. One was the straitjacket escape, but with an added twist. Houdini took the stunt outdoors. He performed it hanging upside down from the outside of a building, forty-five feet above the street!

Houdini stopped traffic with this stunt. Thousands of people jammed the streets to watch. Once, a high wind slammed Houdini into the side of a building. He was badly bruised.

Houdini's daring escapes brought him near death more than once. Many people thought it was only a matter of time before an attempted escape took his life.

Soon Houdini *would* meet his death. But not in the way people imagined.

Chapter Seven

In the fall of 1926, Houdini was performing in Montreal, Canada. Two students came to his dressing room. One had heard that Houdini was strong enough to take any punch.

Before Houdini could prepare himself by clenching his muscles, the student hit him hard in the stomach several times.

Houdini was in severe pain. At the
evening show, he was in a cold sweat. His
temperature was high.

In Detroit the next day, Houdini went
to a doctor. The doctor told him his
appendix had to be removed. After the
operation, Houdini grew even sicker. He
had an infection. Houdini should have
canceled his show, but he didn't. That
night, he went onstage with a temperature
of 104! After the first act, he collapsed
backstage.

Houdini was rushed to the hospital.
But it was too late. He was dying.

Houdini had challenged death many times. He was used to winning. But this time he would lose.

Houdini died in the hospital on October 31—Halloween.

His body was sent back to New York City. It was sent in the bronze coffin Houdini had planned to use in his buried-alive escape!

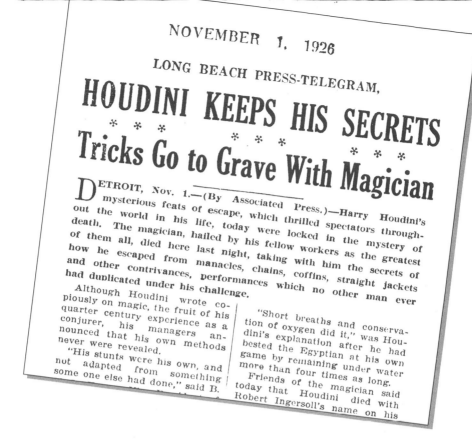

NOVEMBER 1. 1926

LONG BEACH PRESS-TELEGRAM,

HOUDINI KEEPS HIS SECRETS
* * * * * * * * *
Tricks Go to Grave With Magician

DETROIT, Nov. 1.—(By Associated Press.)—Harry Houdini's mysterious feats of escape, which thrilled spectators throughout the world in his life, today were locked in the mystery of death. The magician, hailed by his fellow workers as the greatest of them all, died here last night, taking with him the secrets of how he escaped from manacles, chains, coffins, straight jackets and other contrivances, performances which no other man ever had duplicated under his challenge.

Although Houdini wrote copiously on magic, the fruit of his quarter century experience as a conjurer, his managers announced that his own methods never were revealed.

"His stunts were his own, and not adapted from something some one else had done," said B.

"Short breaths and conservation of oxygen did it," was Houdini's explanation after he had bested the Egyptian at his own game by remaining under water more than four times as long. Friends of the magician said today that Houdini died with Robert Ingersoll's name on his

Newspapers all over America carried the story of Houdini's death. Two thousand people attended his funeral. Outside, thousands more jammed the streets.

There would never be another magician like Houdini. Many believed he had superhuman powers. But Houdini always told them: "There is a trick to everything I do."

Perhaps Houdini's greatest trick was becoming who he was. He was born into a poor family. He was uneducated. But through hard work and determination, he became the world's most famous magician and escape artist. Houdini wrote books, starred in movies, and was the president of the Society of American Magicians.

Once, reporters asked Bess if she knew the secret of Houdini's success.

She replied: "It is Houdini himself. *That* is the secret."

Fluency Fun:

The words in each list below end in the same sounds.
Read the words in a list.
Read them again.
Read them faster.
Try to read all 15 words in one minute.

bee	eat	all
knee	beat	call
see	heat	fall
tree	meat	tall
three	seat	small

Look for these words in the story.

want   **warm**   **color**

winter   **already**

Note to Parents:
According to *A Dictionary of Reading and Related Terms,* fluency is "the ability to read smoothly, easily, and readily with freedom from word-recognition problems." Fluency is necessary for good comprehension and enjoyable reading. The activities on this page include a speed drill and a sight-recognition drill. Speed drills build fluency because they help students rapidly recognize common syllables and spelling patterns in words, and they're fun! Sight-recognition drills help students smoothly and accurately recognize words. Practice these activities with your child to help him or her become a fluent reader.

–**Wiley Blevins,**
Reading Specialist

At last, Ms. Frizzle drove
back to school.

When we came out of the woods,
the bus changed one more time.
It was a Magic School Leaf Blower.

Ralphie's leaf started falling.
But the wind made it float.
It looked like fun.
So we all tried it!

Ralphie ran right into a bird.
Ralphie backed up.

He backed up some more.
He backed right off the branch!

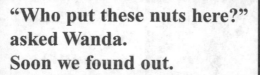

It's fun to be in
Ms. Frizzle's class.

The Magic School Bus®
THE WILD LEAF RIDE

Arnold   Ralphie   Keesha   Phoebe   Carlos   Tim   Wanda   Dorothy Ann

Cartwheel
·B·O·O·K·S·®

SCHOLASTIC INC.

New York   Toronto   London   Auckland   Sydney
Mexico City   New Delhi   Hong Kong   Buenos Aires

Ms. Frizzle   Liz

Written by Judith Stamper.

Illustrations by Carolyn Bracken.

Based on The Magic School Bus books written by Joanna Cole and illustrated by Bruce Degen.

The author and editor would like to thank Dr. Mark Tebbitt of Brooklyn Botanic Garden for his expert advice in reviewing this manuscript.

ISBN 0-439-56988-5

15 14 13   9/0 10/0

Designed by Glenn Davis

Printed in the U.S.A.
First printing, September 2003

Dear Parents,

Welcome to the Scholastic Reader series. We have taken over 80 years of experience with teachers, parents, and children and put it into a program that is designed to match your child's interests and skills.

Level 1—Short sentences and stories made up of words kids can sound out using their phonics skills and words that are important to remember.

Level 2—Longer sentences and stories with words kids need to know and new "big" words that they will want to know.

Level 3—From sentences to paragraphs to longer stories, these books have large "chunks" of texts and are made up of a rich vocabulary.

Level 4—First chapter books with more words and fewer pictures.

It is important that children learn to read well enough to succeed in school and beyond. Here are ideas for reading this book with your child:

- Look at the book together. Encourage your child to read the title and make a prediction about the story.
- Read the book together. Encourage your child to sound out words when appropriate. When your child struggles, you can help by providing the word.
- Encourage your child to retell the story. This is a great way to check for comprehension.
- Have your child take the fluency test on the last page to check progress.

Scholastic Readers are designed to support your child's efforts to learn how to read at every age and every stage. Enjoy helping your child learn to read and love to read.

—**Francie Alexander**
Chief Education Officer
Scholastic Education